EARLY INTERMEDIATE

Schaum Fingerpower POP

LEVEL TWO

10 PIANO SOLOS WITH TECHNIQUE WARM-UPS

Arranged by JAMES POTEAT

The purpose of the Fingerpower Pop series is to provide musical experiences beyond the traditional **Fingerpower®** books. The series offers students a variety of popular tunes, including hits from today's pop charts as well as classic movie themes, beloved Broadway shows, and more! The arrangements progress in order of difficulty, and many include optional accompaniments. In addition, technique warm-ups precede each pop solo.

CONTENTS

ISBN 978-1-5400-3479-3

EXCLUSIVELY DISTRIBUTED BY

Hal•LEONARD®

Visit Hal Leonard Online at
www.halleonard.com

Contact us:
Hal Leonard
7777 West Bluemound Road
Milwaukee, WI 53213
Email: info@halleonard.com

In Europe, contact:
Hal Leonard Europe Limited
42 Wigmore Street
Marylebone, London, W1U 2RN
Email: info@halleonardeurope.com

In Australia, contact:
Hal Leonard Australia Pty. Ltd.
4 Lentara Court
Cheltenham, Victoria, 3192 Australia
Email: info@halleonard.com.au

WARM-UPS

Warm-Ups for
"Colors of the Wind"
(page 14)

1. TWO-NOTE SLURS: 2nds

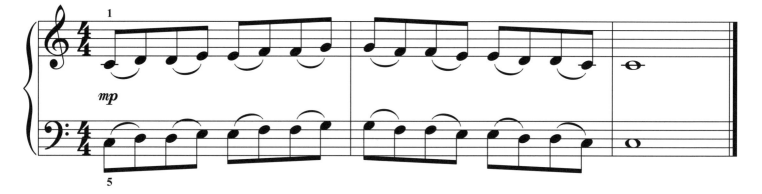

2. TWO-NOTE SLURS: 3rds

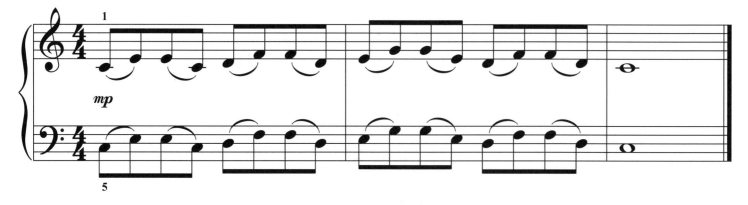

Warm-Up for
"My Heart Will Go On"
(page 16)

WRIST ROTATION

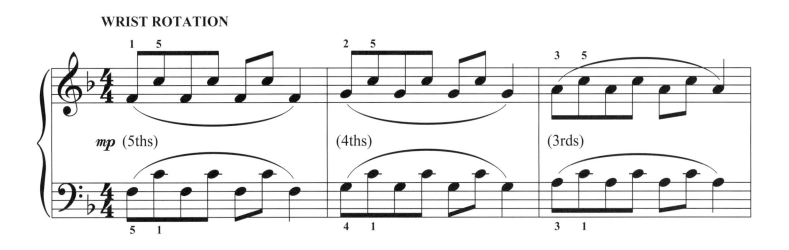

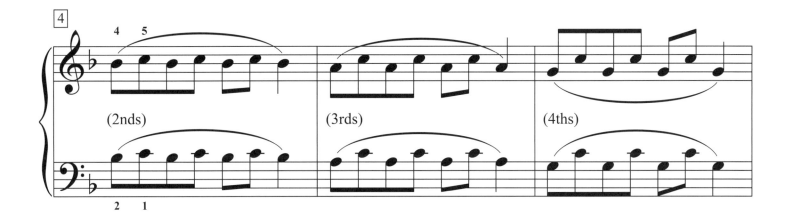

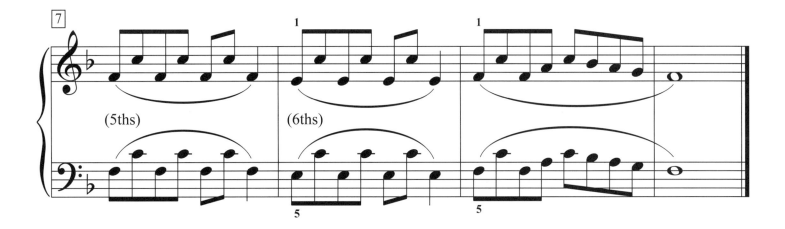

Warm-Up for
"Spongebob Squarepants Theme Song"
(page 18)

"PINEAPPLE UNDER THE SEA"

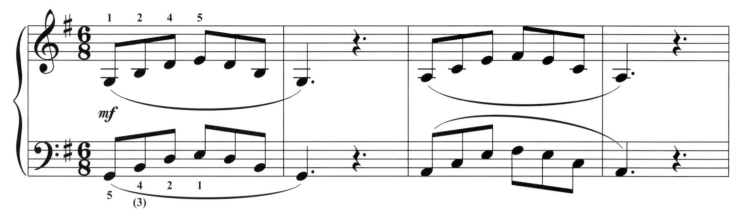

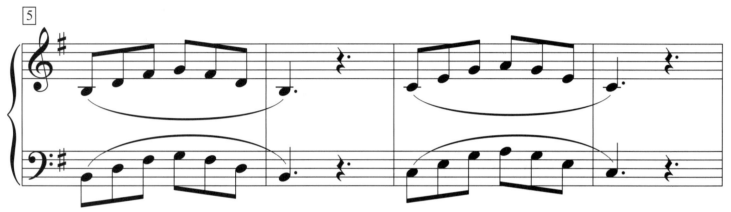

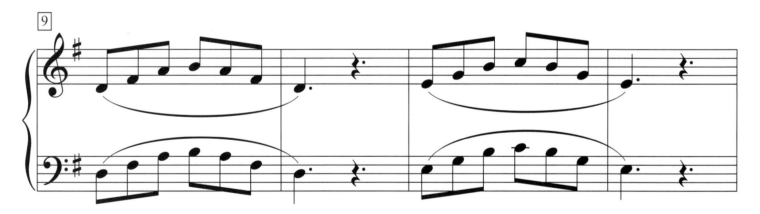

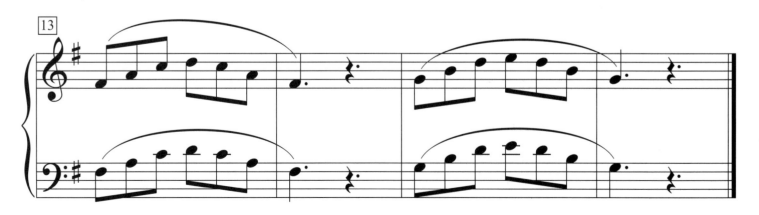

Warm-Up for
"Glad You Came"

(page 20)

ASCENDING & DECENDING OCTAVES in G MINOR

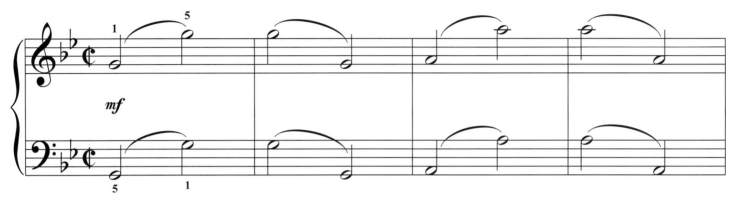

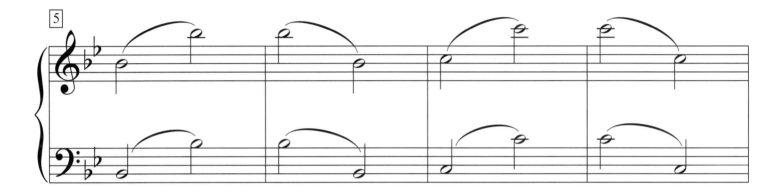

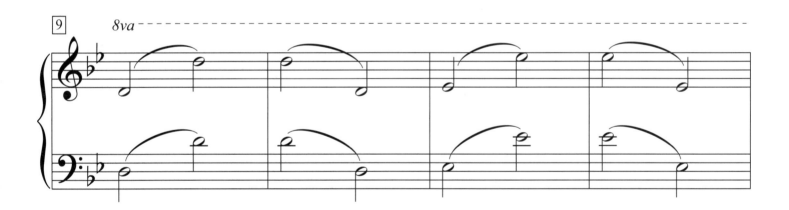

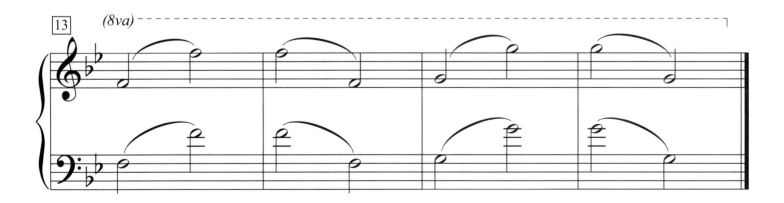

Warm-Ups for
"Stay"
(page 22)

1. FINGER SUBSTITUTION

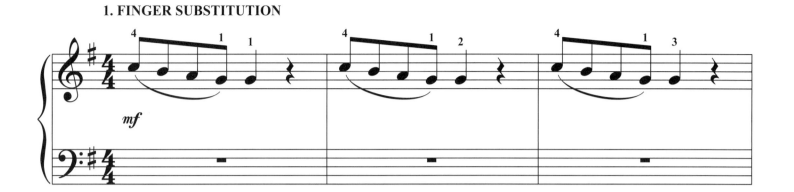

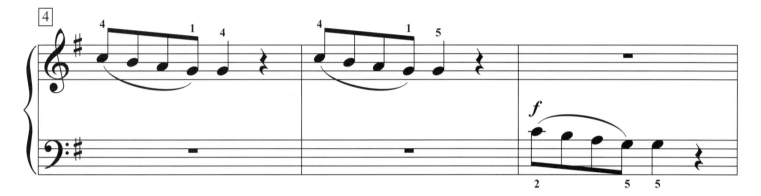

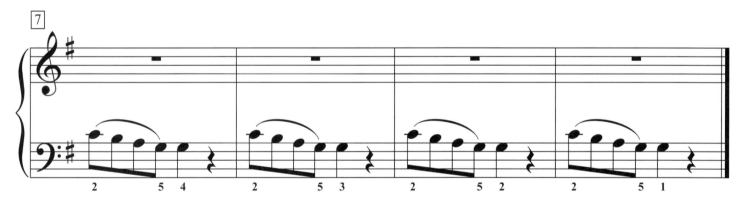

2. RHYTHMIC PEDAL

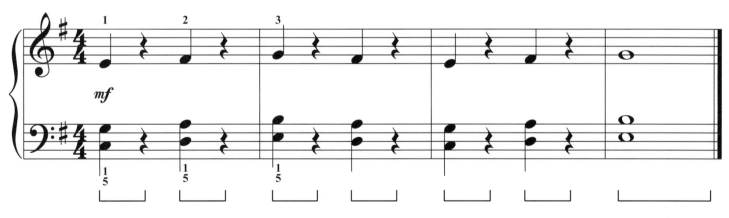

Warm-Ups for
"The Imperial March"
(page 23)

1. EXTENDING THE OUTER FINGERS, L.H.

2. CHROMATIC GROUPS, R.H.

Warm-Ups for
"I Have Confidence"
(page 24)

1. INTERVALS IN THE E-FLAT 5-FINGER SCALE

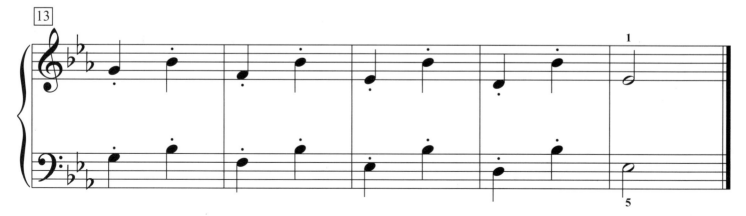

2. SYNCOPATION UP THE SCALE

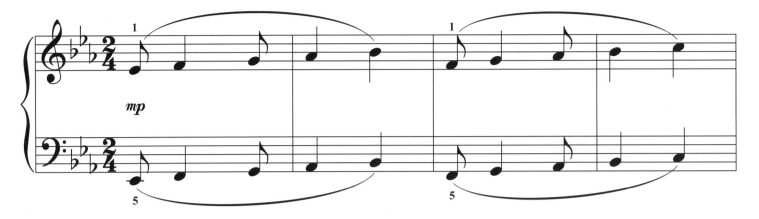

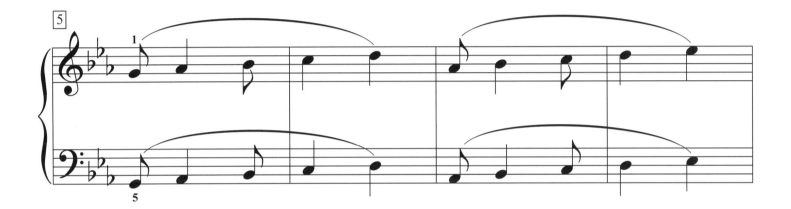

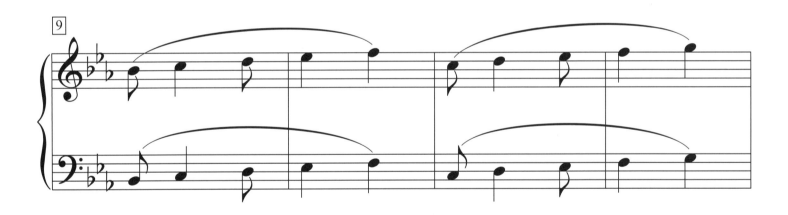

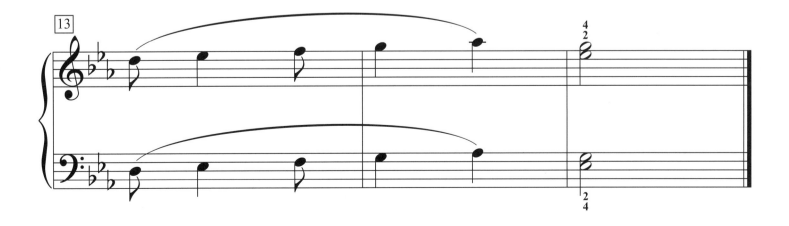

Warm-Up for
"Unchained Melody"
(page 26)

STEPS & SKIPS

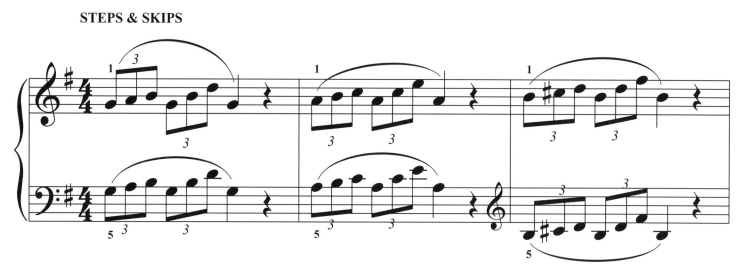

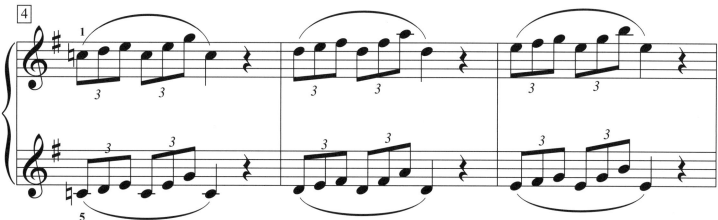

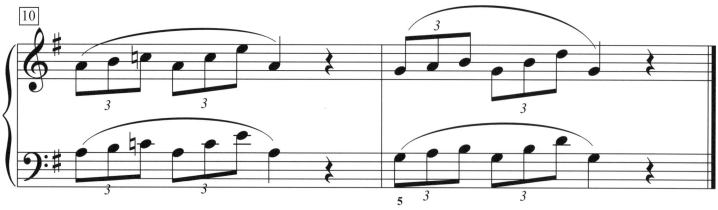

Warm-Ups for
"What the World Needs Now Is Love"
(page 28)

1. BROKEN 7th CHORDS (Swing eighths.)

2. CHORDS WITH SUSPENSIONS (Use pedal.)

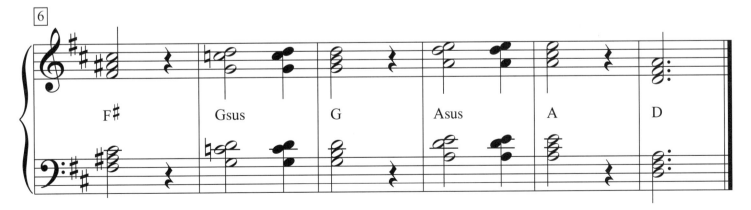

Warm-Up for
"We Are the Champions"

(page 30)

BLOCKED & BROKEN CHORDS
(Pay special attention to the key signature. Use pedal.)

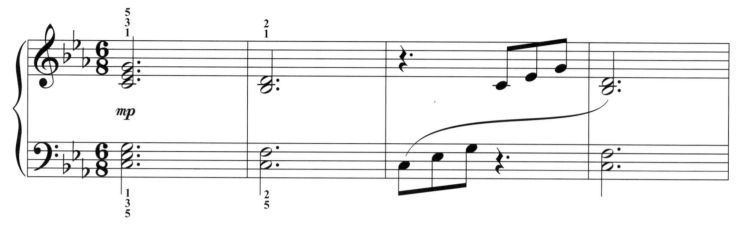

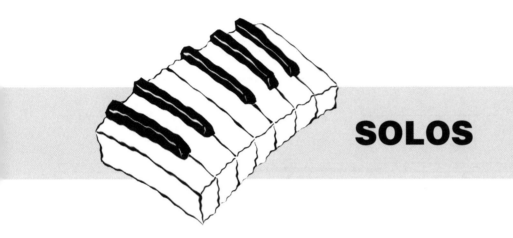

SOLOS

Colors of the Wind
from POCAHONTAS

WARM-UPS: page 2

Music by Alan Menken
Lyrics by Stephen Schwartz
Arranged by James Poteat

Sincerely ♩ = c. 86

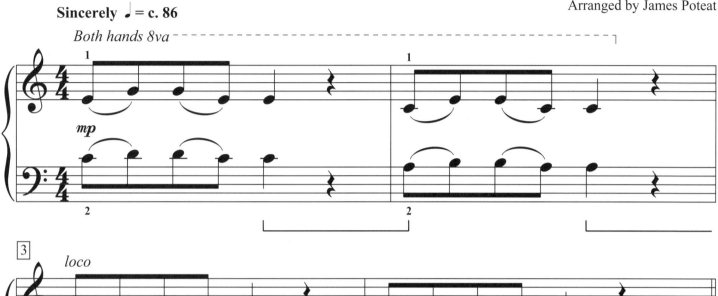

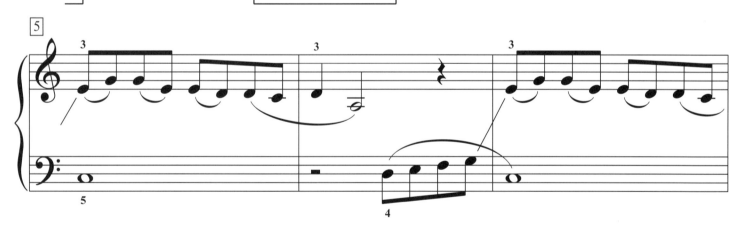

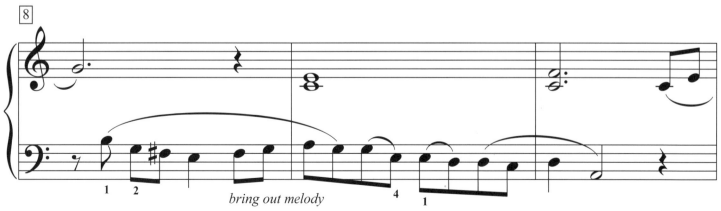

bring out melody

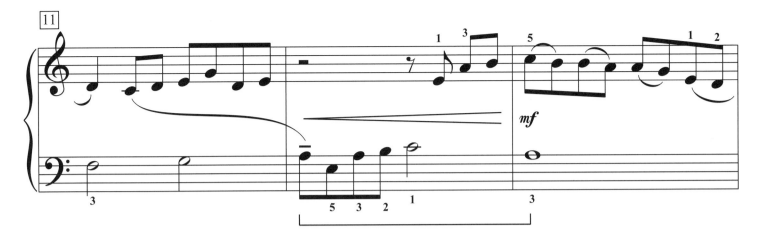

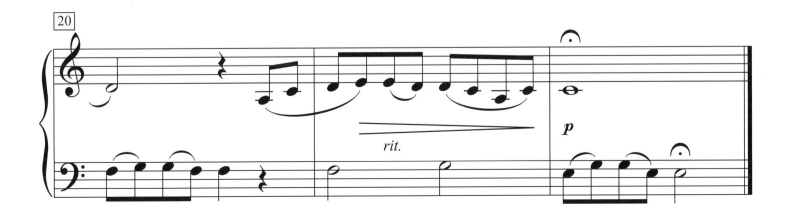

My Heart Will Go On
(Love Theme from 'Titanic')
from the Paramount and Twentieth Century Fox Motion Picture TITANIC

Music by James Horner
Lyric by Will Jennings
Arranged by James Poteat

WARM-UP: page 3

Flowing ♩ = c. 88

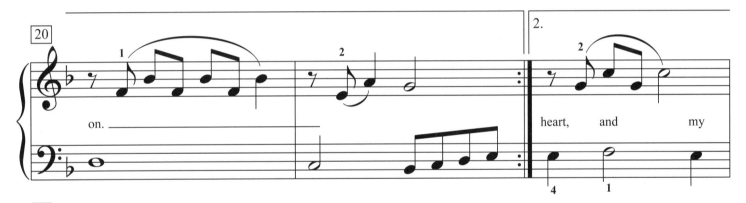

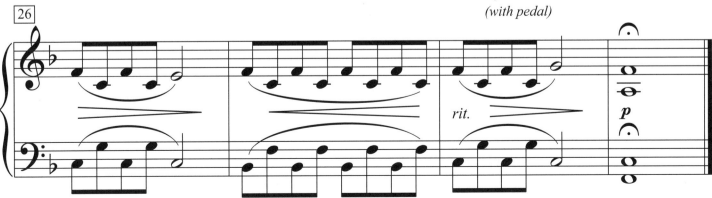

SpongeBob SquarePants Theme Song
from SPONGEBOB SQUAREPANTS

Words and Music by Mark Harrison,
Blaise Smith, Steve Hillenburg
and Derek Drymon
Arranged by James Poteat

WARM-UP: page 4

Peppy ♩. = c. 104

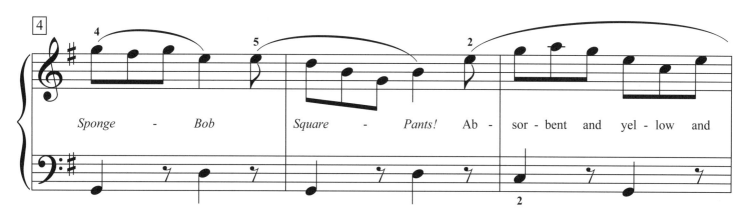

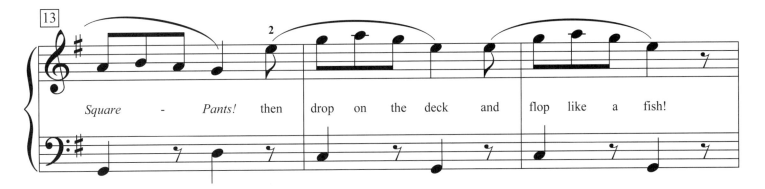

Square - Pants! then drop on the deck and flop like a fish!

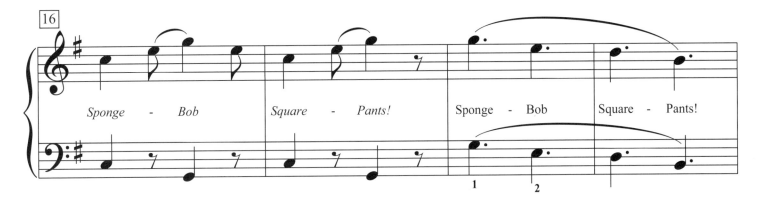

Sponge - Bob   Square - Pants!   Sponge - Bob   Square - Pants!

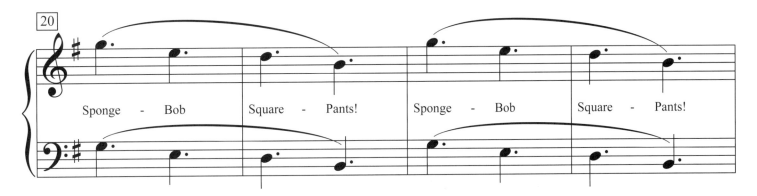

Sponge - Bob   Square - Pants!   Sponge - Bob   Square - Pants!

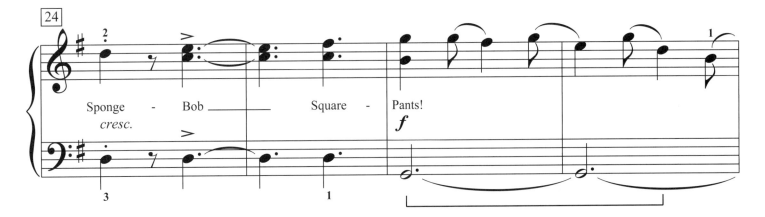

Sponge - Bob _____ Square - Pants!
cresc.   f

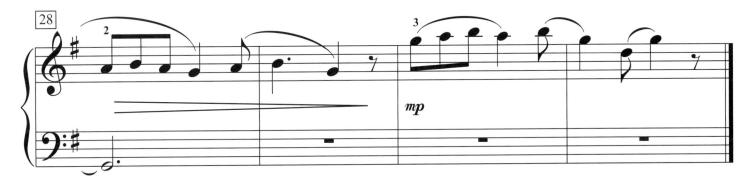

mp

Glad You Came

WARM-UP: page 5

Words and Music by Steve Mac,
Wayne Hector and Edward Drewett
Arranged by James Poteat

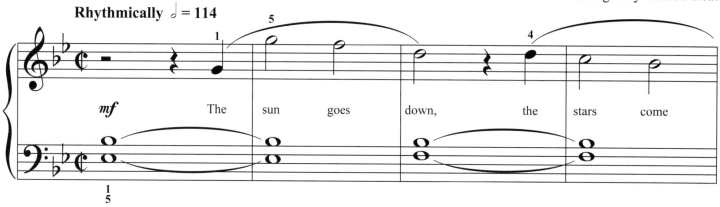

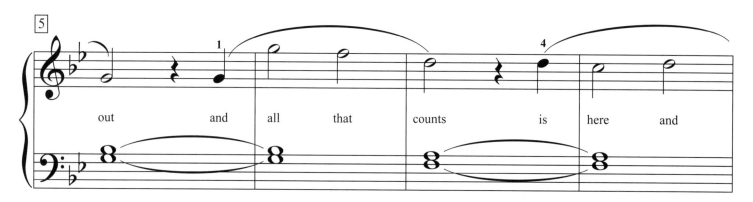

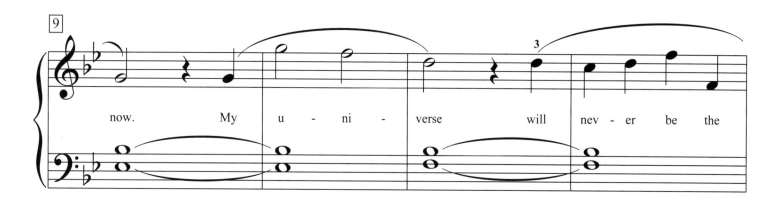

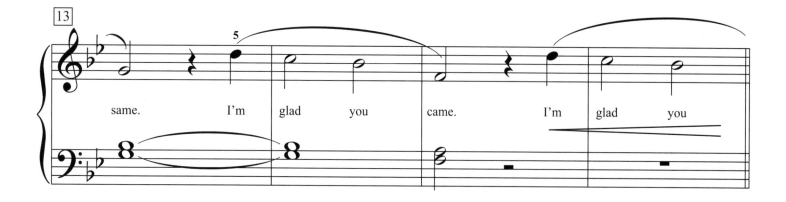

came.

(pedal optional)

simile

Stay

Words and Music by Alessia Caracciolo,
Anders Froen, Jonnali Parmenius, Sarah Aarons,
Anton Zaslavski and Linus Wiklund
Arranged by James Poteat

WARM-UPS: page 6

The Imperial March
(Darth Vader's Theme)
from STAR WARS: THE EMPIRE STRIKES BACK

WARM-UPS: page 7

Music by John Williams
Arranged by James Poteat

Aggressive march ♩ = c. 86

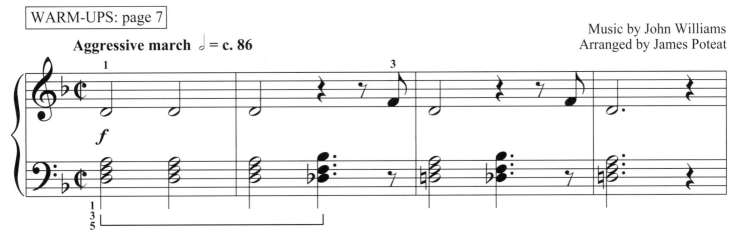

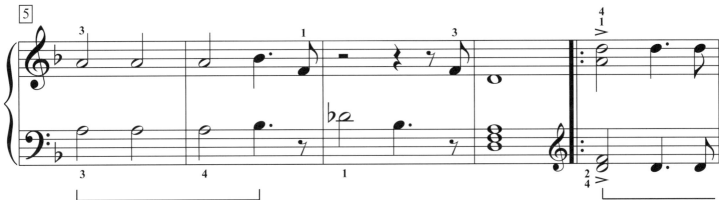

I Have Confidence
from THE SOUND OF MUSIC

Lyrics and Music by
Richard Rodgers
Arranged by James Poteat

WARM-UPS: page 8

Exuberantly ♩ = c. 132

peace - ful slum - bers. When you wake up, wake up! It's health - y.

mf With each step I am more cer - tain ev - 'ry - thing will turn out

fine. I have con - fi - dence the world can all be

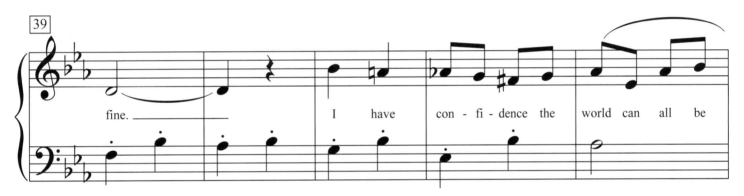

mine. They'll have to a - gree I have con - fi - dence
cresc.

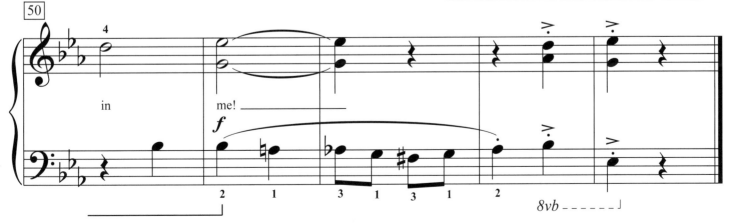

in me! f

8vb

Unchained Melody

WARM-UP: page 10

Lyric by Hy Zaret
Music by Alex North
Arranged by James Poteat

With longing ♩ = c. 76

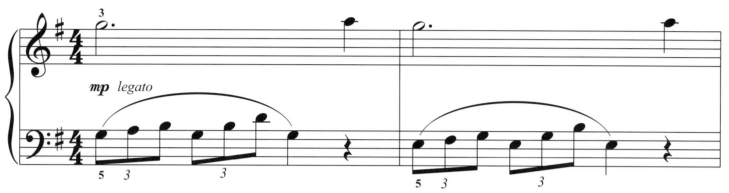

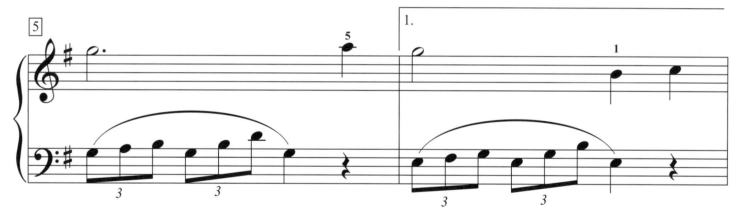

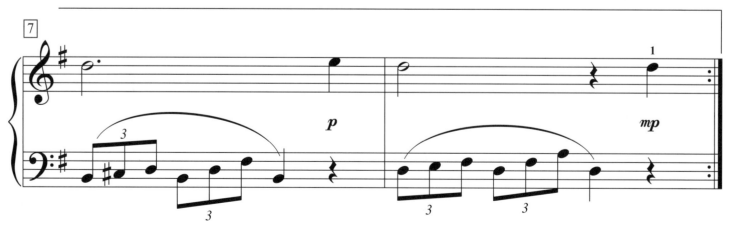

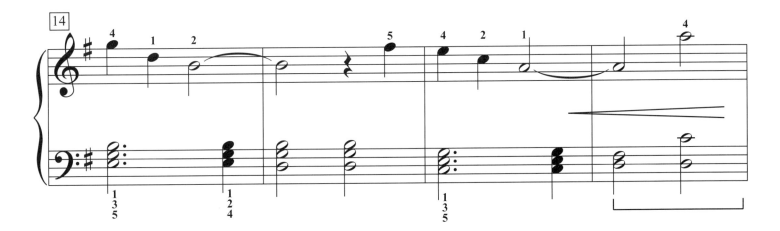

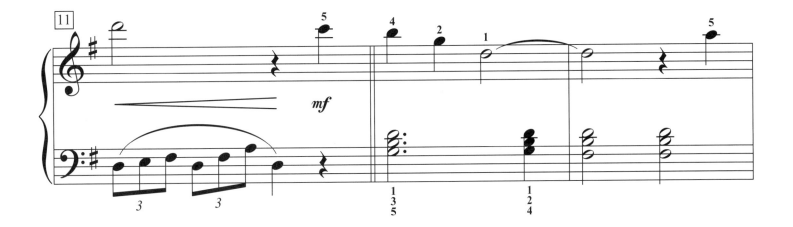

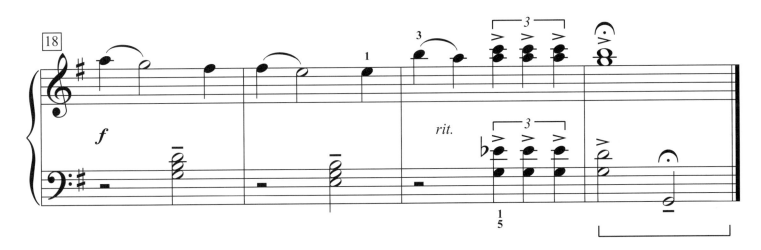

What the World Needs Now Is Love

WARM-UPS: page 11

Lyric by Hal David
Music by Burt Bacharach
Arranged by James Poteat

Tenderly (swing 8ths) ♩ = c. 100

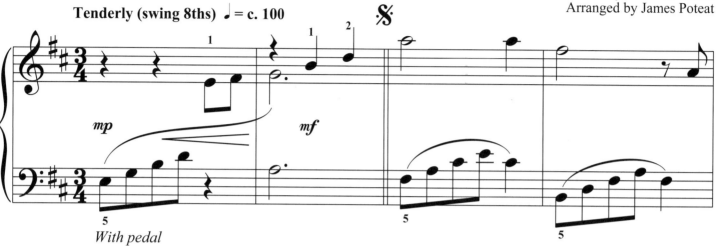

With pedal

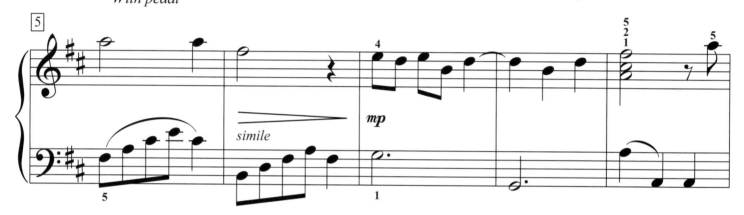

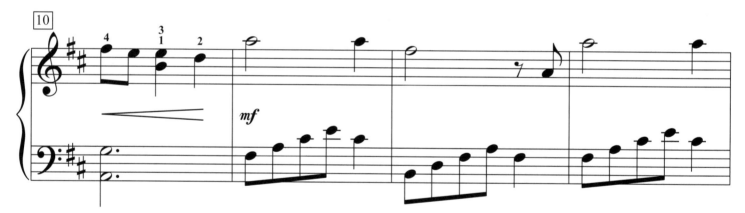

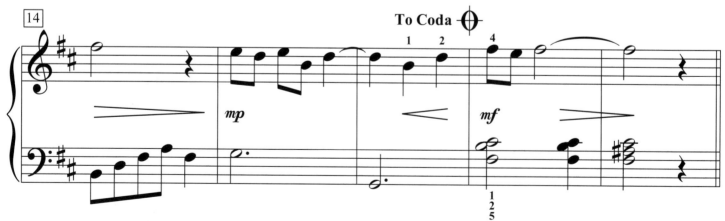

D.S. al Coda

CODA

Slowly

We Are the Champions

Words and Music by
Freddie Mercury
Arranged by James Poteat

WARM-UP: page 12

Moderately slow ♩. = 63

mp

With pedal

simile

mf

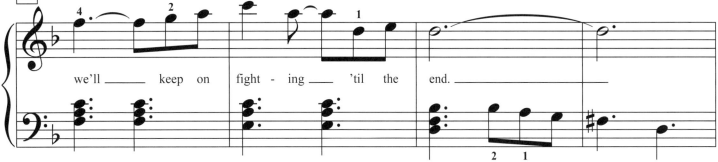

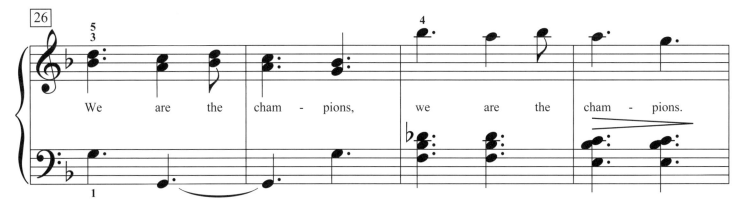

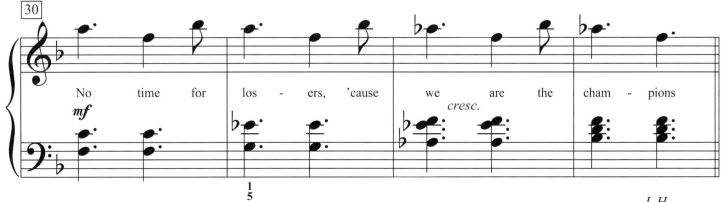

ABOUT THE ARRANGER

Since 2007 **James Poteat** has taught piano, trombone, euphonium, music theory, and composition in Woodstock, Georgia. Mr. Poteat works with students of all ages and skill levels and is equally comfortable in the worlds of popular and classical music. James is constantly arranging music for his students and is dedicated to creating and using materials of the highest quality. Learn more about James and his work by visiting **www.musicalintentions.com**.